LET'S PLAY TAG!

 Read the Page

 Read the Story

 Game

 Repeat

 Stop

INTERNET CONNECTION REQUIRED FOR AUDIO DOWNLOAD.

To use this book with the Tag™ Reader you must download audio from the LeapFrog® Connect Application.
The LeapFrog Connect Application can be installed from the CD provided with your Tag Reader or at leapfrog.com/tag.

BITTEN BY A RADIOACTIVE SPIDER, WHICH GRANTED HIM INCREDIBLE ABILITIES, **PETER PARKER** LEARNED THE ALL-IMPORTANT LESSON, THAT WITH GREAT POWER COMES GREAT RESPONSIBILITY. **AND SO HE BECAME ...** THE AMAZING SPIDER-MAN

SPECTACLED CAIMAN

GALAPAGOS TORTOISE

You're looking for the *Geochelone nigra*, commonly known as the Galapagos Tortoise. It's over there.

If that's what Billy says, you can trust it's right. He's our class reptile expert!

My dad taught me *everything* I know!

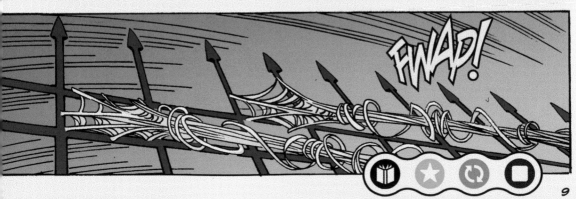

Some reptiles can [re]generate a tail if they lose it. [My] dad was working on a way [to] use lizard DNA and its power of regeneration to help people.

But something went *wrong!*

Let's get to his laboratory!